Bobsled and Luge

BY LAURA HAMILTON WAXMAN

AMICUS HIGH INTEREST • AMICUS INK

Amicus High Interest and Amicus Ink are imprints of Amicus
P.O. Box 1329, Mankato, MN 56002
www.amicuspublishing.us

Library of Congress Cataloging-in-Publication Data
Names: Waxman, Laura Hamilton, author.
Title: Bobsled and luge / by Laura Hamilton Waxman.
Description: Mankato, Minnesota : Amicus High Interest/
Amicus Ink, [2018] | Series: Winter Olympic Sports |
 Includes webography and index. | Audience: Grades: 4 to 6.
Identifiers: LCCN 2016036534 (print) | LCCN 2016039840
(ebook) | ISBN 9781681511504 (library binding) | ISBN
 9781681521817 (paperback) | ISBN 9781681512402
(eBook) | ISBN 9781681512402 (pdf)
Subjects: LCSH: Bobsledding–Competitions–Juvenile literature.
 | Bobsledding–Juvenile literature. | Coasting (Winter sports)–
Juvenile literature. | Winter Olympics–Juvenile literature. |
 Winter sports–Juvenile literature.
Classification: LCC GV856 .W39 2018 (print) | LCC GV856
(ebook) | DDC 796.9/52–dc23
LC record available at https://lccn.loc.gov/2016036534

Editor: Wendy Dieker
Series Designer: Kathleen Petelinsek
Book Designer: Aubrey Harper
Photo Researcher: Holly Young

Photo Credits: Wally Skalij/Los Angeles Times/Getty cover;
Mark Reis/Tribune Content Agency LLC/Alamy Stock Photo
4; Alex Livesey/Getty Images 6-7; PCN Photography/Alamy
Stock Photo 8, 11; Chuck Myers/Tribune Content Agency LLC/
Alamy Stock Photo 12; Erich Schlegel/ZUMA Press/Newscom
15; AP Photo/Dita Alangkara 16; Action Plus Sports Images/
Alamy Stock Photo 19; Chuck Myers/Tribune Content Agency
LLC/Alamy Stock Photo 20, 23; Richard Heathcote/Getty
Images 24; WikiCommons 27; Jens Meyer/Associated Press 28

Printed in the United States of America

HC 10 9 8 7 6 5 4 3
PB 10 9 8 7 6 5 4 3 2

Table of Contents

Katie Uhlaender of the US slides in the 2014 Winter Olympics skeleton.

Going for the Gold

Zoom! A sled flies down an icy track.
Whoosh! It soars around twists and turns.
One woman is on top of the sled. She's
done this many times before. But this is
the Olympics. Will she be fast enough?
The Olympics brings together the best in
luge, bobsled, and skeleton. Every four
years, they race for a gold medal.

Luge, bobsled, and skeleton are sliding sports. They're all about the need for speed. Each racer or team must slide down the track as fast as they can. They get several **runs**. Then all their times are added up. The sliders with the fastest total times win the medals.

This bobsled holds four people. It is designed to go as fast as possible down the track.

Are sliding sports dangerous?

The sliding sports share a long, downhill track. It is around 1 mile (1.6 km) long. But each sport starts their race at a different spot. This icy **chute** is steep and curvy. It has high walls. The racers zoom down it at very high speeds. Every fraction of a second counts. The winner might win by just a **thousandth** of a second!

They can be, especially luge. Sleds can go more than 90 mph (140 km/h). Two luge racers have died in crashes at the Olympics.

Luge

Imagine racing down a mountain on a sled. You're lying flat on your back. And you're going feet first. It's hard to see what's ahead. There are no brakes and no steering wheel. There's no seatbelt either. All you have is a helmet. Welcome to the sport of luge.

Erin Hamlin of the US slides in the luge event in the 2010 Olympics.

Spiked gloves help Christopher Mazdzer of the US push his sled to a fast start.

Q How long has luge been in the Olympics?

Luge racers start out by sitting on their sled. They grab two bars at the starting gate. They rock back and forth to pick up speed. Then they pull themselves forward. Next, they use spiked gloves to push faster on the ice. Then they lie back totally flat. This gives them the most speed down the track. The race is done in under a minute.

 Men's and women's luge have been an Olympic sport since 1964. But the team **relay** is newer. It was added in 2014.

Luge has four **events**. The first two are men's and women's singles. One racer goes at a time. Another event is mixed doubles. One racer lies on top of another. The racing pair can be men, women, or both. But it's usually two men. Why? Men usually weigh more than women. More weight means a faster run.

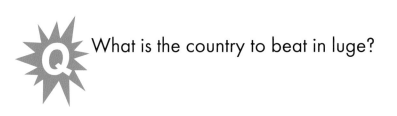 What is the country to beat in luge?

Doubles luge runs can be up to three seconds faster than singles.

Germany seems unbeatable. They often win gold. A German luger has medaled in every luge event since 1964.

The fourth luge event is the mixed team relay. Each team has a woman, man, and doubles pair. The woman goes first. At the finish line, she hits a hanging touch pad. This opens the starting gate at the top. Then it's the man's turn. He does the same thing. The doubles team goes last. Their times are all added together, and the fastest relay team wins gold.

Germany's Natalie Geisenberger hits the touch pad during the 2014 luge relay.

The Skeleton

Skeleton is like the luge. But the sliders lie on their stomachs. They fly down the ice track headfirst. Their chins are just barely above the ice. What a rush! To start, they sprint with their sled. Then they jump on and lie flat. Racers shift their body a little to the right or left to steer. They drag a foot on the ice to slow down.

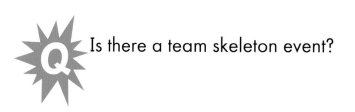 Is there a team skeleton event?

Gold medalist Lizzy Yarnold of Great Britain jumps onto her sled in the 2014 Olympics.

A No. Both men and women have individual events only.

The driver of this US bobsled team watches the track. The others duck down to increase speed.

Q How many women have been on four-person Olympic bobsled teams?

Bobsled

Vroom! Something fast and shiny is racing down the ice track. Is it a rocket? Nope. It's a bobsled. Bobsleds are covered sleds that hold two or four people. Pairs race in the two-man and two-woman events. A team of four races in the four-person event. In the past, only men have competed in this race. But some teams now have a mix of men and women.

 As of the 2014 Olympics, none. But in 2016, at least two women were on national teams. They hope to compete in the 2018 Winter Games.

Bobsled has a fast start. The racers start outside the sled. They grab handles and push the sled out of the gate. Together, they sprint while they push the sled. They build up speed. Then they quickly jump inside.

Once inside the sled, the driver grabs the steering handles. The pushers duck down behind the driver. Zoom!

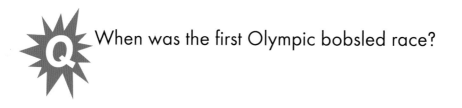 When was the first Olympic bobsled race?

US slider Lauryn Williams and driver Elana Meyers won the silver medal in the 2014 Olympics.

 The four-person race started in 1924. The two-man event was added in 1932. Finally in 2002, the two-woman race was added.

Snow flies as the brake lever is pulled to stop the bobsled at the end of the run.

Now it's all up to the driver. He or she must steer the bobsled just right. Around curves, the sled can't go too high up the track's wall. That will cause it to travel a longer distance. And that loses time. But sticking to the bottom of the track isn't good either. The bobsled will move too slowly around curves.

Winter Thrills

Countries that have a cold, snowy winter do well in the Winter Games. But in 1988, fans got a surprise. A bobsled team from Jamaica **qualified**! Jamaica is a small **tropical** country with no snow. But these athletes found a way to practice with a cart on a paved track.

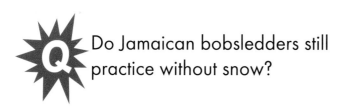 Do Jamaican bobsledders still practice without snow?

Jamaican bobsledders have never medaled. But they are fan favorites.

A No. Since 1997, they have gone to Utah to train on the Olympic track in Park City.

Riding a sled down a hill sounds like fun. But whether athletes are in a wintery or warm climate, they train hard. They need to be strong. They need to run fast. It's hard to find more winter speed. Who will get the fastest start? Who will steer the best? Watch the next Winter Olympics. These sliding sports will thrill you!

US bobsledders celebrate the end of a good run in the 2010 Olympics.

Glossary

chute A long, narrow passage or tube.

event A type of Olympic race, such as singles or mixed doubles.

qualify To do well enough to be able to race at the highest level.

relay A race between teams where each teammate takes a turn doing one part of the race.

run In the sliding sports, one time down the track.

thousandth One part of a second that's divided into one thousand parts; it's faster than a person can blink their eyes.

tropical A place near the equator where it is warm and wet most of the year.

Read More

Hunter, Nick. *The Winter Olympics*. Chicago: Heinemann Library, 2014.

Hunter, Nick. *The World of Olympics*. Chicago: Heinemann Library, 2012.

Johnson, Robin. *Bobsleigh, Luge, and Skeleton*. New York: Crabtree Publishing Co., 2010.

Websites

USA Bobsled and Skeleton
www.teamusa.org/USA-Bobsled-Skeleton-Federation

USA Luge
http://www.teamusa.org/usa-luge

Time for Kids: Winter Olympic Events
www.timeforkids.com/news/winter-olympic-events/137746

Index

About the Author

Laura Hamilton Waxman has written and edited many nonfiction books for children. She loves learning about new things—like sliding sports—and sharing what she's learned with her readers. She lives in St. Paul, Minnesota.